DUBROVNIK

Published by
FORUM - ZADAR
TURISTIČKI INFORMATIVNI CENTAR - DUBROVNIK

Photographs by
MLADEN RADOLOVIĆ
ANDRIJA CARLI
ŽIVKO ŠOKOTA
KREŠIMIR TADIĆ
Archives of the Tourist Union of the City of Dubrovnik
and of Tourist Union of the County of Dubrovnik and Neretva

Editor-in-Chief and Responsible Editor
ĐURĐICA ŠOKOTA

For the Publishers
ŽIVKO ŠOKOTA
NIKOLA BAGARIĆ

Translated by
VJEKOSLAV SUZANIĆ

Computer typesetting by
FORUM - ZADAR

© FORUM - ZADAR, 1999.

CIP - Katalogizacija u publikaciji
Znanstvena knjižnica u Zadru
UDK 908 DUBROVNIK
    930.85(497.5) DUBROVNIK

TRAVIRKA, Antun
    Dubrovnik / written, edited and designed by Antun
Travirka ; [photographs by Mladen Radolović... et
al. ; translated by Vjekoslav Suzanić]. - Zadar : Forum ;
Dubrovnik : TIC, 1999. - 102 str. : ilustr. ; 26 cm

ISBN 953-179-288-7

DUBROVNIK

Written, edited and designed by
ANTUN TRAVIRKA

FORUM
TURISTIČKI INFORMATIVNI CENTAR
DUBROVNIK

Dubrovnik is a city and port on the Croatian coast of the Adriatic Sea. The city has 49,728 inhabitants (1991) and is the economic, cultural and educational centre of southern Dalmatia and the seat of the administration of the County Dubrovnik-Neretva. Besides the area around the mouth of the river Neretva, the county comprises the narrow coast belt which is separated from the interior by the Dinaric mountain range. This range runs in three parallel chains and its height rises towards the interior. The peaks of this range form the natural boundary between the seaboard and Herzegovina, as well as the climatic and anthropogeographical boundary between Dubrovnik and its hinterland.

In the north-western part of the region, the coast belt comprises the Pelješac peninsula, the isthmus of Ston, and the very narrow Dubrovnik seaboard as far as Rijeka Dubrovačka. To the east of the city of Dubrovnik is the coast belt of Župa Dubrovačka along the Gulf of Župa, and to the south-east of the township of Cavtat, the somewhat wider coast belt of Konavle. The Prevlaka peninsula and Point Oštro at the entrance to the gulf of Boka is the southernmost land point of the Dubrovnik region and of the Croatian coast.

A number of islands lie along the coast of the county, from Korčula, Lastovo, and Mljet in the west, continuing with the Elaphite group of in-shore islands - the islands of Olipa, Jakljan, Šipan, Lopud, Koločep and Daksa. The chain ends with Lokrum, which is immediate vicinity - to the south-east right in front of the old city port.

*A view from
Mount Srđ
of Dubrovnik
and its mighty forts*

View of the old port and fortifications

The city of Dubrovnik is situated in 42°40' N and 18°5'E, and is the most southerly Croatian town. Its climate is Mediterranean. Therefore the average yearly temperature is 17°C, characterised by very mild winters and very dry, sunny summer. The average temperature is about 10°C in winter, and about 26°C in the summer. The city is protected from the cold northerly *bura* by mount Srđ, and from the damp southerly *jugo* by the island of Lokrum. Like the rest of the Croatian coast Dubrovnik is refreshed in the summer by the north-westerly breeze *maestra*l. Rains fall mostly in winter, and the snow is seldom recorded. The average summer temperature of the sea is over 21°C.

All these features of climate have resulted in typical Mediterranean vegetation, lush and varied in the coastal belt. It is the result of the action of man who has cultivated this land, reforested it and worked it. It is precisely this combination of natural exuberance and centuries-long activity of the population that have made this region exceptionally beautiful and rich in vegetation.

In addition to the native Mediterranean plants the region abounds in specimens of sub-tropical and continental plants cultivated in numerous gardens and arboretums of the villas scattered all over the coast and the islands. The environs of Dubrovnik get their particular charm from numerous orange and lemon groves, palms and agaves. Many tropical and sub-tropical plants and trees have been brought by seamen from their distant voyages. Close to the city, in the residential areas which

Placa (Stradun), view of Luža, the Bell Tower and the House of the Main Guard

cluster round the old historic city, but also in other areas in the vicinity (Trsteno, Lopud, Lapad, Lokrum, Cavtat), flowers are cultivated in private gardens and other horticultural areas, giving these areas a special atmosphere from early spring until late autumn.

The varied geomorphology of the region - steep rocky coast, deep coves, sandy beaches, small fields, high mountains which in places come right to the sea, numerous islands and rocks, together with the rich vegetation and exceptionally clear sea - all this makes the region very attractive. Man has been civilizing the environment for centuries. Man and nature have worked together, combining natural beauty, architecture and horticulture. The

result of this happy connection is one of the most beautiful and impressive regions, not only on the Croatian coast and the whole of the Adriatic area but also one of the best cultivated oases of the Mediterranean.

With the exception of the area of the Neretva estuary and the island of Korčula, the territory of the present-day county is the same as the territory of the former Republic of Dubrovnik. With an area of 1375 sq. km it was among the smallest but very important merchant republics of the Mediterranean. Its role of linking the commercial routes between eastern and western Adriatic areas, and between the eastern and western parts of the Mediterranean was of great importance, particularly from

the 14th to the 17th century. The centre of this republic, a city-state, was Dubrovnik.

Dubrovnik arose in a very significant place. Close to the shore and right in front of the city is the island of Lokrum, the last in the series of many islands of the east Adriatic. To the south-east spreads the wide open sea, leading on to the Strait of Otranto and to the vast area of the Mediterranean sea. Towards the north-east, near the coast, island groups form protected channels, suitable for navigation of ships. In immediate vicinity of Dubrovnik, the Dinaric range becomes lower, allowing mountain passes over which caravan roads towards the interior could be organised. A city in such a position had to be predestined for navigation and sea trade, and natural barriers separated and protected it from the neighbouring geographic and geopolitical units.

The beginnings of Dubrovnik fall in the relatively distant past and - like many old Mediterranean cities - are veiled in legend. Among several legends about its origin, historically the most credible is the one linking the foundation of the new city with the destruction and fall of the Roman city of Epidaurum (at the site of present-day Cavtat) in the 7th century. Epidaurum was a very old settlement. It was very probably founded as a Greek colony, although there are no certain finds. In Roman times it was a developed town and an important sea-trading emporium. It is presumed that it suffered heavily from an earthquake in the 4th century, when parts of the city fell into the sea, but it continued its existence as an important centre. It was also mentioned as the seat of a bishop. In 614 Epidaurum was captured and destroyed by the Avars and Slavs, and the survivors fled to the nearby woods and to a small rocky islet named Laus. *Laus* or *Lave* is 'rock' in Greek, *labes* is 'sheer slope' or 'chasm' in Latin, which describes a locality which obviously had a steep coast, a cliff. The islet was separated from dry land by a narrow channel so

Stroll in front of Sponza palace

Yachting regatta before the walls of Dubrovnik

that the settlement on it was protected from both sea and land. The rock was probably inhabited even before the arrival of refugees from Epidaurum, and the newcomers only increased the number of inhabitants. The latest archaeological excavations, particularly the discovery of the first cathedral from the 7th century, seem to corroborate this fact. The fate of Epidaurum and the origins of Dubrovnik show historical similarity to the origins of Venice and Split. Venice came into being because the refugees from Aquileia fled to the marshlands of the lagoon before Attila's Huns in the 5th century, and Split began in the 7th century after the destruction of Salona by the Avars and Slavs when the refugees found shelter in the

fortified palace of the Roman Emperor Diocletian. The city which rose on Lausa took its name from it: *Rausa, Ragusa* and *Ragusium*. It is obvious that in the 9th century Dubrovnik was a highly organised municipal unit with a system of protective ramparts because it successfully resisted a 15-month siege of the Saracens. The city was aided in defence by the Byzantine fleet. From the 7th to the 12th century the city grew under the domination of Byzantium. As with many other seaside communes ruled by Byzantium, aspirations towards autonomy gradually grew stronger, leading to the development of commerce and related activities. In the meantime, a Croatian settlement developed on the mainland opposite Ragusa, which was named

Splendid view of the island of Lokrum and Župa Dubrovačka bay from the walls

Dubrovnik, probably after the groves of holm-oak (*dubrava* in Croatian). Links between the two settlement became stronger with time, which resulted in a mixed Croatian and Latin population. The channel between the islet and the mainland had become silted in the course of the 10th and 11th centuries, and was filled with carted material at the close of the 11th century. The widest and most famous street in the city - Placa (Stradun) - runs today in the place where the islet was joined to firm land. Both parts were finally integrated in the 12th century: they were protected by a system of defence walls. The northern suburb was also included in the 13th century, the streets were regulated, and Dubrovnik acquired its present shape. The first records of Dubrovnik's name occur in the documents issued by the Bosnian ruler Kulin in 1189. He gave preferential treatment to the merchants of Dubrovnik. The same name is recorded in the chronicle written by the so-called Priest of Dioclea (Pop Dukljanin) in the 12th century. The fact that the Latin speaking people on the islet of Lausa were isolated among the Croatian majority is proof of a relatively speedy assimilation and the domination of the Croatian element, much sooner and to a higher degree than in other Dalmatian cities which were part of the Byzantine Theme. By the 14th city was Croatized completely. This fact will be crucial for the flowering of Croatian literature in the city of Dubrovnik.

In 1032 the ships of Dubrovnik joined the fleet of Byzantium in the war against the Arabs. In 1153 the Arabian author Al-Idrisi describes Dubrovnik as the southernmost city in Croatia, a city owning many ships which sail on distant voyages. Dubrovnik and Pisa signed a contract in 1169 regulating sea trade in the Mediterranean sea from Pisa to Constaninople. By the end of the 12th century Dubrovnik negotiated contracts with many Adriatic cities: Molfetta, Ravenna, Fano, Ancona, Monopoli, Bari, Tremoli and with Rovinj and Kotor. Dubrovnik made very important commercial arrangements with its land neighbours, Bosnia and Serbia, ensuring for itself in this way the status of the principal commercial emporium for these Balkan countries.

In the 12th century Dubrovnik was ruled by a rector elected by the citizens. His decisions were crucial for functioning and development of the city. This period saw changes in the structure of Dubrovnik, and a class of noblemen landowners was established. They gradually assumed all administrative functions in the city, which now developed as a typical Mediterranean aristocratic republic. With its successfully organized sea trade Dubrovnik now competed with Venice, which used all methods to check her rising rival. In 1205 Dubrovnik came under Venetian authority.

Venice ruled Dubrovnik for the next 150 years, which left a fairly strong imprint on the social structure of the city. Dubrovnik was forced to accept the rector and the bishop from Venice. She also nominated the members of the Major Council, and made every effort to acquire full power in the city. In the 13th century Dubrovnik attempted to defect on several occasions. Although the development of the city was slowed, Venice could never acquire complete control over its trade. In the same century, in addition to numerous agreements with Italian and Croatian coastal cities, Dubrovnik

Rijeka Dubrovačka, Villa Sorkočević

A motif from the island of Lopud

established commercial relations with Epirus and Albania, and also extended its trade to Syria and northern Africa.

Trade brought many foreigners and foreign ships to Dubrovnik, and Dubrovnik was compelled to hire foreign ships for its ever-growing business. Yet with all this large volume of sea trade in the period of Venetian domination, connections with the interior of the Balkans were much more important.

Dubrovnik acquired the Island of Lastovo in 1252, the Pelješac Peninsula in 1333, and the Island of Mljet in 1345.

With the peace treaty of Zadar in 1358, Dubrovnik was freed of the Venetian supremacy for she was forced to renounce her possession on the east coast of the Adriatic. From then Dubrovnik acknowledged the supreme authority of the Hungaro-Croatian kings. This would influence the future development of the city. These kings never interfered in the administration of the city, its commercial and sea affairs, which resulted in full autonomy of the free and sovereign aristocratic republic. Thus the earlier title of COMMUNITAS RAGUSINA (The Municipality of Dubrovnik) was replaced by RESPUBLICA RAGUSINA (The Republic of Dubrovnik). In 1399 the Republic gained the

Picturesque Suđurađ on the island of Šipan

coastal belt from Ston to Orašac, and in 1419 and 1427 it reached its final size - when it acquired Konavle and Cavtat. Growing unrest and disorder in the Balkans forced Dubrovnik to turn to sea trade.

Withdrawal of Venetian ships from joint ventures gave impetus to shipbuilding and almost complete dependence on own ships. In the 14th and the 15th century the trade of Dubrovnik spread to Egypt, Syria and Sicily, but also to the ports of Aragon in Spain and to France. In the 15th century, Turkey rose as a naval power in the Mediterranean, and Dubrovnik established exceptional commercial relations with Turkey, at the same time paying Turkey tribute for trading privileges.

In 1526, after the battle of Mohács, when the Turks defeated the Hungaro-Croatian army, Dubrovnik stopped paying tribute to the Hungaro-Croatian kings, and their authority over Dubrovnik was over. Dubrovnik maintained particularly careful relations with Turkey, paying them tribute. The Turks did not interfere in the internal affairs of Dubrovnik, but - in addition to regular tribute - they exacted various gifts and bribes.

In the centuries of its greatest power, Dubrovnik was a typical aristocratic republic. All power was in the hands of the patricians. They had become a closed social class in the first half of the 14th century. The urban society was divided into three classes: the patricians, the "good citizens", and the commoners. The patricians had exclusive right to political power, and because of power they acquired all the land. Their multiplied continuously, and in mid 16th century their number rose almost to 1500 members. The most prestigious families formed an oligarchy which played crucial role in politics and state business. The so-called "good citizens" were a thin layer of the richest merchants, who were financially equal to the patricians but did not share political power with them. Small merchants, craftsmen, workshop labourers , boys and sailors formed the general layer of the population. In mid 16th century Dubrovnik had 4000 sailors. The Republic had passed laws forbidding sailors to sign on foreign ships. Social stratification of the rural areas varied from bondsmen to sharecroppers to yeomen on the island of Lastovo. Irrespective of the great need for sailors, the Republic did not allow villagers to sign on ships lest the drain of manpower should result in neglect of agriculture.

The Jewish community enjoyed special status. They were active in finance and trade, but they were also physicians. The Jewish community lived in the ghetto, but fairly free. They worshipped in the synagogue which was the only non-Catholic temple in the Republic. As Dubrovnik was a developing society, living in relative comfort, the patricians ruled without oppression.

The Republic was ruled by three councils headed by the rector whose term of office was one month only, and who had the same rights as all other members. The Major Council was composed of all adult patrician males. They elected the Senate and the Minor Council. Real power was held by the Senate. Until 1491 it had 51 members, later 61. The

Neptune's fountain in the garden of Villa Gučetić at Trsteno

Above: Defence wall and forts of Mali Ston   *Following pages: The fortified city of Ston and the salt pans*

Minor Council was in fact the executive authority, being an organ of the Senate and the Major Council. The term of office of all the organs of the Republic was one year. The judiciary was controlled by the Senate and the Minor Council. All major posts in the government and in the administration of justice were held by the patricians; ordinary citizens and commoners filled insignificant offices only. Occasional exceptions can be met in the diplomacy and consular functions. The territory of the Republic was divided in 12 administrative units.

In the golden age of the Republic its material riches were based on widespread production and transfer of silver and lead from Bosnian and Serbian mines to the developed areas of Europe where demand for these metals was enormous. The merchants of Dubrovnik had indeed concentrated considerable trade with these mineral products in their hands. They leased and even owned some mines, they organised production and transport of metals to the port of Dubrovnik and then re-exported it to Florence, Venice, Spain and France. In order to promote functioning of these

important activities, the businessmen of Dubrovnik organised a number of colonies at key points of the caravan trails. This important activity had ceased completely after the Turkish conquest of Serbia and Bosnia. The same happened to the production of textile. The trade in silver had enabled the purchase of high quality wool from Catalonia, which was used to manufacture and dye cloth of high quality in the workshops in Pile, Rijeka Dubrovačka and Župa Dubrovačka. The

Above: The island of Mljet, remains of the Early Christian basilica at Polače   *Right: Lastovo*

textiles manufactured in these workshops were competitive on foreign markets. However, Turkish conquests stopped purchases of raw materials, and because of immediate Turkish danger, the Republic decided in 1463 to pull down all the workshops outside the city, so that this production came to a standstill. Dubrovnik maintained its salt monopoly in the area between the Neretva and the Drin rivers, which made the Balkan countries dependent. The craftsmen of Dubrovnik now turned to supplying local markets, but a modest trade in leather goods and gold was somehow maintained. Commerce, sea-trade and shipbuilding became the most important activities after the Turkish conquests of the Balkans. The shipbuilders of Dubrovnik were far known, so ships built "in the manner of Dubrovnik" meant durable, strong and simple construction. In mid 16th century Dubrovnik owned over 180 large ships with total burden of 36000 *"kola"*. This fleet was valued at about 700,000 ducats. Credit transactions and naval insurance brought great profits. Dubrovnik passed law on naval insurance as early as 1568. Its ships sailed as far as England, but the discovery of new naval routes to India round Africa severed the trade in spices in the Levant. Like other Mediterranean trading republics, Dubrovnik was hit by ever-growing recession caused by the discovery of

Above and right: Cavtat, the seaboard centre of Konavle

America and new sea routes to Asia. But the merchants of Dubrovnik found ways to master these problems. Thus Vice Bune, master mariner of Dubrovnik, entered Spanish service and in the late 16th century, sailed to East India and invested his money in the port of Goa.

That Dubrovnik trade was extensive in spite of recession at the close of the 18th century can be seen from the fact that Dubrovnik had consulates in over 80 cities, among them Lisbon, Madrid, Gibraltar, Malaga, Tangier, Barcelona, Marseilles, Nice, Mayorca, Tunis, Tripoli, Genoa, Leghorn, Venice, Pesaro, Ancona, Naples, Palermo, Malta, Alger, Brindisi, Taranto, Triest, Rijeka, Shkodra,

Durrës, Vlorë, Corfu, Thessaloniki, Varna, Constantinople, Smyrna, Latakia, Rhodos, Alexandria, Cyprus etc. The fleet, including the fishing boats, totalled 673 sailing ships, of which 255 larger ships sailed to foreign waters, and 230 were ocean ships. These data show clearly the size and strength of Dubrovnik's commerce and navigation, even in the period of decline. In its most glorious days the fleet of Dubrovnik was equal to that of Venice, but incomparably weaker than the fleet of the Netherlands.

Political activities of all men who filled offices in the Republic and all their private interests and ethical norms were subordinated to the welfare of

Above:
Konavle, the falls of the Ljuta

Right:
Konavle, the beach below Popovići

the state. Because of its size and delicate strategic position, the Republic relied most heavily on the diplomatic ability of its representatives and ambassadors. Centuries of diplomatic experience in extremely complex political conditions had created in Dubrovnik one of the most subtle schools of diplomatic business in the world. The ability of its ambassadors is even now the subject of scholarly and practical research. The fact that Dubrovnik had never fought a war of aggression but had acquired new territory, that it maintained trade relationships with the Levant - with Pope's permission - in the times of most violent wars between Christians and Moslems, that it never took part in any action of the allies against the Turks, that it maintained trade relations with Turkey throughout its existence, that in spite of direct military threats from the Balkan countries and the Turkish empire, and in permanent danger from Venice, it never fought war after early 15th century - all this is the best proof of the skill of its diplomacy. Even when completely destroyed by earthquake, Dubrovnik successfully averted the immediate danger from the Turks and Venice because of the ability and courage of its diplomats. There are many examples, in the history of diplomacy, of ability, of

courage, and of sacrifice for the welfare of the Republic. It may be of interest to know that the Republic was among the first countries of Europe to recognize the United States officially.

Long peaceful periods in the history of Dubrovnik and the relative bounty in which the city lived made it possible for science and art to flourish. Renaissance was especially fruitful in literature. The first 15th century poets to distinguish themselves writing in Latin were Karlo Pucić, Jakov Bunić and the famous poet laureate Ilija Crijević who was crowned with laurel in Rome in 1485. But early 15th century also saw first attempts to write verse in Croatian. Đono Kalić wrote some Croatian verse in 1421, but it was only the Petrarchan tradition that created lyric poetry in the Croatian language. The early Renaissance poetry by Džore Držić and Šiško Menčetić deserves especial note. The first stage attempts were made by Mavro Vetranović, followed by the comedies of Nikola Nalješković, and in mid 16th century came the

dramatic work of Marin Držić, which has almost no contemporary match in Europe for its scope, imaginativeness and poetic quality. The same could be said of the famous Baroque poet Ivan Gundulić, the author of the splendid epic "Osman" and of the most beautiful verse on freedom ever written. Many scientists and scholars lived in Dubrovnik - the historian Ludovik Crijević Tuberon, Benko Kotruljić, who wrote a book on commerce in 1573, Nikola Sagrojević, who studied the phenomena of the tides, the mathematician, physicist and opticians Marin Getaldić and the greatest of them all: physicist, mathematician and philosopher Ruđer Bošković, one of the greatest minds of the Baroque period, whose works presents some ideas that are current even today.

Dubrovnik had outstanding painters in the 15th and 16th centuries. Numerous painters' workshops flourished in those times. Unfortunately, first the earthquake and then the fires have destroyed most of the production. Few unharmed paintings

Beneath the arches of Sponza palace

Dominican monastery, Nikola Božidarević, Dubrovnik, detail of triptych, 16th century

survived to the present day, and they testify to a production of high quality, which shifted from international Gothic towards Renaissance. Worth mentioning are the paintings by Lovro Dobričević, by his son Vicko Dobričević, by Mihajlo Hamzić, and by the brilliant Renaissance painter Nikola Božidarević whose four polyptychs represent the peak of the Renaissance painting school in Dubrovnik.

The most tragic event which occurred in Dubrovnik in its whole history was a devastating earthquake on April 6, 1667. More than 5000 citizens died under the ruins of their city. One of the most beautiful and harmonious cities of the Mediterranean vanished in ruins and fires which ravaged what was left of the city for days. The whole historic centre, its beautiful Romanesque cathedral and the representative Gothic and Renaissance palaces, churches and monasteries were turned into an irreparable pile of debris. There were losses even among the ships in the port. Dubrovnik recovered slowly and with difficulty.

The city changed completely. Instead of the characteristic Gothic and Renaissance house fronts and the architectural vividness which occurs when a city grows and develops in centuries of peace and prosperity, Dubrovnik was now rebuilt in stern and modest Baroque houses of the same appearance and design, with compulsory shops on the ground-floor. All the representative sacral buildings that had been destroyed were now renewed in the Roman Baroque style. The Sponza Palace alone has preserved its original shape, and partly the front of the Rector's Palace. Fortunately, most of the fortifications had withstood the devastating force of the earthquake, except for minor damage. But even with such changes in its outlook, Dubrovnik has remained one of the most beautiful and architecturally most precious urban units in the Mediterranean.

The Republic did not die because of historical wear: it was abolished in 1808 as an act of Napoleon's occupying power. After the fall of Napoleon hopes were nurtured that the Congress of Vienna would renew the Republic, but the Austrian imperial authorities opposed it because of their pretensions to extend their rule to the whole eastern Adriatic territory. Within the Austrian empire Dubrovnik led an empty existence as a provincial town of Dalmatia, only its shipping remained important. Social disintegration brought decay and total collapse of the gentry. This decay described

Dominican monastery, Nikola Božidarević, The Annunciation, 1513

by Ivo Vojnović, the great writer and playwright from Dubrovnik. Between the two wars, Dubrovnik lived mostly from its shipping, but also from tourism which developed systematically.

After 1950, Dubrovnik experienced sudden increase of the tourist industry. Many new hotels were built, to be followed by entire tourist villages in the immediate vicinity. The new airport at Čilipi (Konavle) has considerably advanced and accelerated the development of tourism. In the late nineteen-eighties Dubrovnik was one of the most prized tourist destinations in Europe. The ideal combination of natural beauty, cultural heritage and entertainment was attracting thousands of tourists.

Since the free elections of 1990 Dubrovnik has been one of the most important cities of the independent Croatia. But before it had achieved full freedom it had to go through the most difficult temptations. In the autumn of 1991, the Yugoslav People's Army launched a most brutal and criminal attack against the city and the unarmed civilians. For months, they ravaged, looted, burned and thoroughly destroyed what man had created in the area. Having devastated Konavle, the coastal belt and Župa Dubrovačka, the enemy attacked the city and its cultural and art heritage. The bestial shelling of the city, recorded by TV cameras and broadcast to the world, warned the world about the horrible war in the very heart of Europe.

Having withstood the siege, Dubrovnik survived the terror. Wounded but proud, Dubrovnik is recovering in free Croatia, and tourists are coming again to see its walls and palaces. Dubrovnik is now the pride of Croatia and a true jewel of Europe.

The most recognizable feature which defines the physiognomy of the historic city of Dubrovnik and gives it its characteristic appearance, famous all over the world, are its intact *city walls*, which run uninterrupted for 1940 metres encircling the city. This complex structure, one of the most beautiful and strongest fort systems in the Mediterranean, consists of a series of forts, bastions, casemates, towers and detached forts. The walls were built systematically in the difficult times of permanent danger to the City and the Republic, and they have been preserved to the present day and are still functional, not only because of the proficiency of their skillful builders, diligence and care of the citizens of Dubrovnik who maintained them and added to them as necessary, but also because of the splendid ability of the famous diplomats who knew how to obviate and avert the dangerous intents of the enemies and rivals of the Republic. The city of Dubrovnik is completely surrounded with walls and forts, including the Old Port. The history of the fortifications goes back to the early Middle Ages. No doubt the earliest urban settlement upon the islet of Laus was protected by walls. The fact that the city was able to resist the Saracens who besieged the city for fifteen months in the 9th century means that it was fortified well. The city first spread towards the uninhabited eastern part of the islet. The present name Pustijerna for the southeastern end of the city close to the Fortress of St. John, derives from the Latin expression *post terra* which could be freely translated as "outskirts". This eastern section was included within the defence walls in the 9th and 10th century. When the sea channel which separated the city from firm land was filled with earth in the 11th century, the city merged with the settlement on land and soon a single wall was built around the area of the present-day city core. The whole city was enclosed by walls in the 13th century, except for the Dominican monastery, which came under their protection only in the 14th century. The average thickness of the wall was 1.5 metres, and it was built of stone and lime. To increase the strength of the wall and ensure better defence, 15 square forts were built in the 14th century. Extensive work was done on the walls towards the close of the 14th century, at the time of the final liberation from the Venetian supremacy. The sudden danger from the attacks of the Turks after the fall of Constantinople in 1453, coupled with the simultaneous latent threat from

Strong land walls dominated by the tower Minčeta

Venice gave the greatest stimulus to further reconstruction and urgent repair of the fortifications. Owing to the enormous efforts of the citizens and noblemen, as well as the skill of many urgently hired fort builders, most of the forts were strengthened, especially the ones towards the mainland, and new forts and semicircular bastions before the walls were completed in less than three years. The system was extended and modernized during the 16th century, even later. The design of the walls derives from the 14th century, while the definite shape was fixed in the period which is, not without reason, referred to as the Golden Age of Dubrovnik, i.e. from the fall of Constantinople in 1453 until the devastating earthquake of 1667. The main wall on the land side is 4 to 6 metres thick, but narrower on the side facing the sea - 1.5 to 3 metres thick. Its height reaches 25 metres in some places. The wall on the land side is protected by an additional scarp wall as defence against artillery fire. The irregular quadrilateral formed by the walls is protected at four prominent points by strong forts. The strong round Tower Minčeta is to the north, the port is protected by the detached Fortress Revelin in the east and by the big complex of the Fortress of Saint John in the south-east. The western entrance to the city is protected by the strong and beautiful tower Bokar. The western end of the city is also protected from danger from the sea and land by the powerful detached Fortress Lovrijenac. In addition to these strong and most prominent fortifications, the city walls are protected

additionally by two round towers, 12 quadrilateral forts, 5 bastions and two corner towers, while the scarp wall is flanked by one large and 9 semicircular bastions. Along the part of the wall facing inland a deep ditch was dug as additional protection. The whole system was furnished with a large number of guns. They were mostly cast in local workshops, which were famous in these parts. The most prominent 16th century cannon designer and producer in Dubrovnik was Ivan of Rab. In times of full alert Dubrovnik was defended by over 120 artillery pieces. The city maintained communication with the outer world by means of two well protected gates, situated east and west. Entry from the west was through the fortified and well protected Pile Gate (Vrata od Pila), while the eastern Ploče Gate (Vrata od Ploča) was additionally protected by the detached fortress Revelin. Both entrances were constructed in such a way that communication with the city was not direct, but anyone entering the city was forced to pass through several gates and winding lanes, which testifies to cautionary measures against sudden raids or entry of undesirable visitors. Entry to the port, a most important area of this commercial and maritime city, was through two gates: the Port Gate (Vrata od Ponte) and the Fish Market Gate. The port was protected from the force of the waves or sudden attack from the sea by the breakwater named Kaše. The whole network of streets was subordinated to quick and purposeful communication with the forts. Nowadays, a walk upon the city walls is an attraction for tourists. Such a walk can best reveal the fabric of old Dubrovnik, because different points offer new vistas. It is particularly the higher parts that reveal many picturesque details, as well as the general lay of the city and its streets, squares and widenings, which cannot be visualised during a

Michelozzo di Bartolomeo and Juraj Dalmatinac, the tower Minčeta, 15th century

walk along the streets. In addition to unforgettable views of the city, such a walk will offer a magnificent view of the open sea before Dubrovnik and of the immediate surroundings. A walk along the city walls can start from two points. In the east the entry is near the Bell tower, and in the west near the Church of the Saviour, at the Pile Gate.

The most prominent point in the defence system toward the land is the round *tower Minčeta*. The name derives from the name of the Menčetić family, who owned the ground the tower was built upon. By its height and impressive volume the tower dominates the north-western high part of the city and the walls. It was built in 1319, originally as a strong four-sided fort. It was built by a local builder Nićifor Ranjina. As the fall of Constantinople in 1453 was a clear sign to the cautious citizen of Dubrovnik quickly to take ample defensive measures, the first and one of the most important tasks was to strengthen this key point. The fall of Bosnia, which followed soon in 1463, only hastened the works. The Republic invited a famous architect, Michelozzo di Bartolomeo of Florence. His work in Dubrovnik resulted in several buildings of highest importance for the defence of Dubrovnik. Among his principal activities around the middle of the 15th century was the reconstruction of the tower Minčeta. Around the earlier quadrilateral fort Michelozzo built a new round tower adapted to the new technique of warfare and joined it to the new system of low scarp walls. The walls of the new tower were full 6 metres thick and had a series of protected gun ports. The work on Minčeta was continued by the famous architect and sculptor Juraj Dalmatinac, born in Zadar. He designed and built the high narrow round tower, while the battlements are a later addition. The tower was completed in 1464, and is the symbol of

the unconquerable city of Dubrovnik. Since it is the highest point of the wall, it offers an unforgettable view on the city.

In the period of unmistakable Turkish danger and the fall of Bosnia under Turkish rule, *the fortress Revelin* was built to the east of the city in 1462, a detached fortress providing additional protection to the land approach to the eastern Ploče Gate. The name derives from *rivelino* (ravelin), a term in military architecture which refers to work built opposite to the city gate in order to afford better protection from enemy attack. Danger of Venetian assault suddenly increased in the times of the First Holy League, and it was necessary to strengthen this vulnerable point of the city fortifications. The Senate hired Antonio Ferramolino, an experienced builder of fortresses in the service of the Spanish admiral Doria, a trusted friend of the Republic. In 1538 the Senate approved his drawings of the new, much stronger Revelin. It took eleven years to build it, and during that time all other construction work in the city had stopped in order to finish this fortress as soon as possible. The new Revelin became the strongest city fortress, safeguarding the eastern land approach to the city. It is an irregular quadrilateral, with one of its sides descending towards the sea, and protected by a deep ditch on the other sides. One bridge crossing the protective ditch connects it to the Ploče Gate, and another connects it to the eastern suburb. The construction work was executed perfectly so that Revelin was not harmed by the devastating earthquake of 1667. As its interior is divided into three large vaulted rooms, Revelin became the administration centre of the Republic. The sessions of the Councils were held in the fortress, and the treasuries of the Republic and of the Cathedral were transferred there, and so was all other wealth which was saved from the ruins and fires following the earthquake.

The top of Revelin is a huge stone terrace, the largest in Dubrovnik, used in summer as a stage for many events of the summer festival.

Left:
Fort Revelin protected the eastern gate.

Old port and the forts Revelin and St. John

The Fortress of St. John, often called *Mulo Tower*, is a complex monumental building on the southeastern side of the *Old City Port*, controlling and protecting its entrance. The first fort was built in mid 14th century, but it was modified on several occasions in the course of the 15th and 16th centuries, which can be seen in the triptych by the painter Nikola Božidarević in the Dominican monastery. The painting shows St. Blasius, the patron saint of Dubrovnik. In his hands he holds a scale model of Dubrovnik where the fortifications of the port can be seen clearly.

The present appearance of the fortress dates from the 16th century and is mainly the work of the local builder Paskoje Miličević, whose reconstruction plans contributed considerably to the present look of the fortification of the Old Port. The side towards the sea is round and the lower part of the wall is inclined, while the part facing the has flat vertical walls. This large building, which had many gun ports for its primary function, is a cultural monument today. It houses the *Maritime Museum*, containing objects, paintings and documents relating to a most important activity in the history of the city. The ground-floor houses the famous *Aquarium*. The monumental space of the fortress creates a special mood for visitors who can view specimens of Adriatic fauna in 27 basins of various sizes.

The opposite side of the old port was protected by the *Fortress of St. Luke*, built in the 14th century, and the city engineer Paskoje Miličević added a round bastion to it. Prior to the building of the

The walls from the sea. Left: Fortress Lovrijenac, centre: Fortress of the Passing Bell

breakwater the old port was closed at night by a chain and wooden beams which were stretched between the Forts of St. John and St. Luke.

Construction of the breakwater named Kaše started in 1484 from the drawings of the same engineer. This object offered protection to the port from southerly winds, and it added substantially to the safety of the anchorage against possible raids from the sea.

The Arsenal was situated in the port. It consisted of four separate vaulted areas where the galleys for the defence of the city were docked. Warships for immediate defence of the city were built and maintained there. The Republic owned no other warships, but their merchant ships were armed adequately. The Arsenal was often modified over the centuries, it was reconstructed or new parts were added. A fact testifying to the proverbial caution of the Republic ought to be mentioned. If a new construction or a long repair was started, the arched openings were walled in. The walls were knocked down and opened again when the vessel was completed in order to launch it. The arsenal serves nowadays as the well-known *coffee house*, its three semicircular arches looking towards the port.

The southern section of the walls rises over steep cliffs which precipitate into the sea. This section was not much affected in the general reconstruction of fortifications in 15th and 16th centuries.

Following pages:
A view of the old port and the fortress of St. John

Among the rare additions was the round fortress on the most outstanding point of the southern wing of the wall. *The Fortress of the Passing Bell* was built early in the 16th century according to the plans drawn by the local builder Paskoje Miličević. Because of a large number of gun ports it was the focal point of defence between the tower Bokar and the fortress of St. John against possible danger from the sea. It was named after the bell in the nearby church of St. Peter which announced citizens' deaths.

The tower Bokar (Zvjezdan) is among the most beautiful instances of harmonious and functional fortification architecture. It was built by the above mentioned Michelozzo of Florence while the city walls were reconstructed (from 1461 to 1463). This tower was conceived as the key point in the defence of the Pile Gate, i.e. the western fortified entrance to the city. Together with Minčeta this tower is the second key point in the defence of the western land approach to the city. It was built as a two-story casemate fortress, standing in front of the medieval wall face and protruding into space almost with its whole cylindrical volume. Nowadays the tower is used as a stage for events in the summer festival of Dubrovnik.

The famous *fortress Lovrijenac* was built upon a sheer rock 37 metre high overlooking the sea. This detached fortress is of prime importance for the defence of the western part of Dubrovnik, both against attack from land and the threat from the sea. The fortress was mentioned in a legend from the 11th century, but reliable data are from the 14th century, when its present form was determined. It was reconstructed several times in the centuries that followed. The main reconstruction occurred together with other fortresses: in the 15th and 16th centuries. In those times the municipal builder I. K. Zanchi of Pesaro was repairing the parapets. Having suffered damage in the earthquake of 1667, Lovrijenac was also repaired in the 17th century. Triangular in plan and following the contour of the rock on which it was built,

Lovrijenac faces the western suburbs with its narrowest, highest part, and its longest wall is open towards the tower Bokar and the western wall, thus protecting the small, but also the oldest port of the city - Kolorina. The fortress has a quadrilateral court with mighty arches. As the height is uneven, it has three terraces with powerful parapets, the broadest looking south towards the sea. Lovrijenac was defended with 10 large cannons, the largest and most famous being *Gušter* (Lizard). It never fired a single shot. It was designed and cast in 1537 by master Ivan of Rab. As it is a dominant fortress whose capture could endanger the City and the Republic, its construction reveals all the wisdom and caution of the administration again. The walls exposed to enemy fire are almost 12 metres thick, but the large wall surface facing the city does not exceed 60 centimetres. The caution of the Republic was not only directed against the foreign enemy, but also against possible mutiny of the commander of the garrison of the fortress. Therefore the would-be tyrant was permanently exposed to the threat of destruction of the thinnest wall of the fortress. As caution was never sufficient, the commander of the fortress, always elected from the rank of the nobility, was replaced every month. The Republic defended freedom in every possible way. The famous inscription over the entrance to Lovrijenac: NON BENE PRO TOTO LIBERTAS VENDITUR AURO is witness to that. In translation: Freedom is not sold for all the gold in the world.

In the search for space suitable for theatre productions during the summer festival, it was observed very early that the three terraces of this fortress has great potential. It is especially suitable as the stage for Shakespeare's "Hamlet", and its production at Lovrijenac has become cultic and the trade mark of the summer festival.

*Right: The mighty fortress Lovrijenac,
one of defence pillars of Dubrovnik*

The Pile Gate has been the main entrance to the city for centuries, and the whole area outside the walls was so named (from Greek *Pyle*, "gate"). The gate got its present shape in 1537 when the outer semi-circular tower with a Renaissance arch was built and the statue of St. Blasius, the patron saint of Dubrovnik, was set in a richly decorated niche. The approach to the gate is over a stone bridge and a wooden drawbridge, suspended by chains, which was lifted every evening with great ceremony. The first stone bridge was built in 1397 by Giovanni of Sienna, while the later, longer bridge with several arches, was built from the drawings of the famous architect Paskoje Miličević. This bridge spanned the deep protective ditch which was dug systematically along the city walls. The inner gate was built

Mask from the Big Onofrio fountain

place where

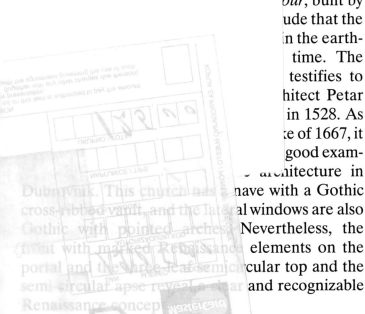

can Monas-
our, built by
ude that the
in the earth-
time. The
testifies to
hitect Petar
in 1528. As
e of 1667, it
good exam-
architecture in
nave with a Gothic
al windows are also
Nevertheless, the
elements on the
cular top and the
and recognizable

close to the city
the inner Pile Gate. It was built in late 13th and early 14th centuries. It was one of the most respectable convents in the Republic. A home for foundlings was founded in this

Left: Pile gate

convent as early as 1434 to care for abandoned and illegitimate babies. It was one of the first institutions of its kind in the world. The children were nursed in this home up to their sixth year and than entrusted to the care of decent families.

The French authorities dissolved the convent and turned the building into ammunition depot and later into horse stable.

In the middle of a small but pleasant square close to Pile Gate is the *Big Onofrio's fountain*. It was built in 1438 by the Neapolitan builder Onofrio della Cava who was hired by the Republic to construct the urban aqueduct. While the majority of Dalmatian cities under Venetian authority solved the problem of water supply by building large cisterns for rain water, Dubrovnik decided to bring water from a well. Dubrovnik aqueduct from the late Middle Ages is an exceptional case. Onofrio tapped the well named Šumet at Rijeka Dubrovačka, 12 kilometres away from the city. He built two branches at Konali above the city itself. One branch supplied the workshops in the Pile area, and the other turned to the city at the level of the tower Minčeta. Onofrio also built a number of mills along this branch. The water thus brought to the city was accessible to the public in two places:

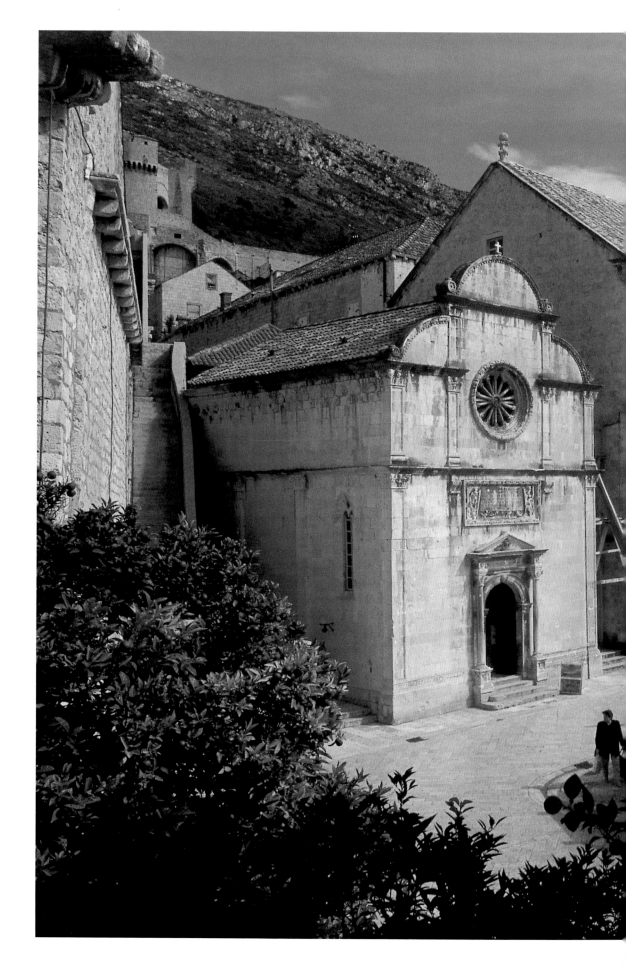

A picturesque square near the western gate, the church of the Saviour, the Franciscan monastery and the Big Onofrio fountain

Stradun (Placa), view towards Franciscan monastery

at a large polygonal fountain with a water reservoir which he built close to the western gate, and at a smaller fountain in the east which supplied the market place at Luža square. In addition to these two main fountains there were several others: at the fish-market, in the port, in the atrium of the Rector's Palace, and in the cloister of the Franciscan Monastery. A smaller fountain for the Jewish community was also built.

For its form and volume, set in a small quadrilateral square, the Big Onofrio's fountain looks like a replica of a former Romanesque baptistery of the former cathedral in Bunić's Square. This fountain was heavily damaged by earthquake in 1667 and what we see today is a bare architectural volume whereas the splendid sculptural ornaments are lost

forever. The original 16 masks in relief are still extant and water jets are gushing out of their mouths.

Placa is the main open urban area in Dubrovnik and the most favoured promenade and gathering place. It is the venue of all popular feasts and processions, but also the main business street of the old city centre. This widest and most beautiful street divides the old city into northern and southern halves. At the same time it is the shortest communication between the western and the eastern gates. This street was created at the close of the 11th century when the shallow channel separating the islet of Lava and the settlement upon it from the settlement on mainland was filled with earth in order to join them. Placa acquired its proper function at the close of the 12th century when both floor, which shows that the authorities cared about maintaining business life. Notwithstanding its modesty, this new complex cannot be denied certain harmony or rhythm of volumes nor the dignity of clean stone walls.

The large complex of the *Franciscan monastery (Friars Minor)* is situated at the very beginning of Placa, to the left of the Pile Gate. The lateral façade of the monastery church runs along the principal street of Dubrovnik, and the monastery spreads north along the walls as far as the tower Minčeta. The earliest monastery was built in the 13th century in the Pile area. As the city was threatened with war, in 14th century the friars were forced to move under the protection of the defence walls. The new monastery building was started in 1317 but work went on for a very long time. Some parts were destroyed and rebuilt several times. The large Franciscan church, one of the richest churches in Dubrovnik at the time, was destroyed in the earthquake of 1667. The only element of the former building which has been preserved is the portal on

Brothers Petrović,
The portal of the Franciscan church, 15th century

Following pages:
The cloister and garden of the Franciscan monastery

Below: Capitals shaped like dogs (14th century)

settlements were enclosed by a single city wall and became one urban whole. The name Placa is derived from the Greek and Latin *Platea*, which we translate as "street". The other name, *Stradun*, is a Venetian sobriquet used ironically in the sense of "Big street". The present shape was acquired after the earthquake of 1667 ·when Dubrovnik was hastily rebuilt after destruction and fires. The picturesque diversity of the former palaces of old Placa was replaced by planned and unified construction of two rows of stone houses built in the Baroque style, of equal height with similar fronts and similar internal arrangement. The Senate of the Republic had ruled that every house should have space for several shops on the ground-

Franciscan pharmacy, one of the oldest in the world

the south wall. It was probably moved from the front to the lateral wall in the course of the restoration in the 17th century. According to the contract of 1498, this portal, the most monumental one in Dubrovnik at that time, was carved in the leading local workshop owned by the brothers Leonard and Petar Petrović. The portal has all the marks of the Gothic style, but the solid volumes of the figures show the Renaissance spirit. The figures of St. Jerome and St. John the Baptist are set above the door-posts, while the Pietŕ in relief is represented in the central Gothic lunette. The figure of the Father Creator is above the lunette. Such iconography of the portal and the choice of the patron saints are proof of the aspirations and social doctrine of the Franciscan in the political circumstances of the times. St. John the Baptist symbolizes Christian constancy in the face of the Turkish penetration. St. Jerome symbolizes the spiritual unity with the rest of Dalmatia. The Pietŕ symbolizes their compassion with the poorest members of the urban community who sought solace from the Franciscans anyhow, and the figure of the Creator on top should symbolize opposition to the humanist world-views of the time. The church was reconstructed in the Baroque style. The northern wall of the church closes the southern wing of one of the most beautiful cloisters of Dubrovnik. This cloister was built in late Romanesque style by master Mihoje Brajkov of Bar in 1360. The ambient is most harmonious, framed by a colonnade of double hexaphoras, each with a completely different capital. The Franciscan cloister is one of the most valuable late Romanesque creations on the Croatian shores of the Adriatic. The Franciscan monastery has another cloister built in the Gothic style, but it is for private use only and not accessible to the public.

A *pharmacy* was founded in the monastery 1317, the third oldest in the whole world, continuously functioning until the present day. The monastery owns one of the richest old libraries in the Croatia, famous all over the world for the value of its inventory. The collection has over 20,000 books, over 1200 of which are old manuscripts of extraordinary value and importance, 137 incunables and seven books of old church corals. The collection of liturgical and art objects is exhibited in the large Renaissance hall, containing the inventory of the old Franciscan pharmacy, paintings by old masters, valuable specimens of gold-work and rare books.

The eastern widening of Placa - *the Luža Square* - formerly was used as market place. The famous Roland's column soars in the middle of the square and a great number of most important administrative and sacral buildings are situated around the square, such as the Baroque church of St. Blasius, the patron saint of the city of Dubrovnik, the Palace of the Major Council, the building of the Main Guard, the Little Onofrio's Fountain, the Bell Tower, the bell house Luža, and the Sponza Palace, seat of the Custom-House and the Mint. The main festivities take place on Luža square, such as the feast of St. Blasius or the opening ceremony of the summer festival.

The great theatre and music festival under the title of *Dubrovnik Summer Festival* has taken place without interruption since 1950. The programme takes place between July 11 and August 25 on 33 open-air stages in the city. Owing to original historic places of old Dubrovnik, which are natural stages for many drama productions on account of their picturesque character, and places that become ideal for music productions on account of extraordinary acoustic properties - such the atrium of the Rector's Palace or the marvellous churches - the festival is known all over the world as a festival which attracts famous names of the theatre and music. The ambience is so much charged with historic meaning, artistic values and unmatched natural beauty that it is almost an ideal framework for artistic pleasure of the highest level. The spectacular opening of the festival on July 10 is particularly impressive. The whole city and all the visitors take part in it. The focal ceremony of this unique night takes place in Luža Square, when Festival flag is hoisted on Roland's column.

The Baroque *church of St. Blasius*, the patron saint of Dubrovnik, was built in 1715 in the place of the former Romanesque church which was consecrated to the same saint. This precious building was badly damaged by earthquake in 1667, and completely destroyed by fire in the night of May 24/25, 1706. The Senate hired the Venetian architect Marino Gropelli, who built the present church on the model of the Venetian church of St. Mauritius. It is a central building with an oblong cupola in the centre, a large portal with rich ornaments, and a broad flight of stairs before the entrance. The rich outer Baroque ornament is in sharp contrast with the severe, simple house fronts in Placa, but it refreshes the ambience in a way.

The interior of the church is richly decorated according to the norms of its representative Baroque style. The magnificent altars built in coloured marble are most pronounced in this respect. The high altar has a precious Gothic statue of St. Blasius in gilt silver, made in the 15th century by an unknown master of the local school. Because of its high

Interior of the church of St. Blasius, 18th century

quality it is one of the most precious statues in the long history of art in Dubrovnik. In addition to its art value, this statue is also a historical document because the in his left hand saint holds a scale model of Dubrovnik showing the buildings which were later destroyed by earthquake. Of the many gold and silver statues and church vessels, this was the only statue to survive the fire, and this fact was taken as the proof of its miraculous power.

St. Blasius (Vlaho) is to Dubrovnik what St. Mark is to Venice. *The feast of St. Blasius*, the Patron saint, is observed every year on February 3, and it is the true feast of the whole city. It is known far and wide for its pageantry and participation of people from neighbouring villages in their picturesque costumes, for its majestic procession in which the relics of the Saint are carried, and for popular events and merrymaking. In the times of the

Left: The Church of St. Blasius

Republic it was a custom seven days before the feast and seven days after it to release from jail prisoners who were not dangerous, and anyone who was permanently banned from the city could come back for the festivities. St. Blasius was bishop of Sebasta in Armenia, he suffered martyrdom under emperor Diocletian, and became patron saint of Dubrovnik in the 10th century. It seems that he appeared in a dream to one Stojko, rector of the cathedral, and warned him that the Venetians, anchored near the island of Lokrum, intended to attack the city that night. After the Senate had meticulously checked Stojko's report, St. Blasius became the patron saint of the city of Dubrovnik. His statue was carved on all fortresses of the city and above all gates of Dubrovnik. St. Blasius also adorns the flag of the Republic, and the figure of the bearded bishop with mitre and pastoral staff appeared on all official seals of Dubrovnik and on coins minted in Dubrovnik.

Left and below:
Procession on St. Blasius' day, principal feast of the city

In the space between the Rector's Palace and the bell tower stood formerly the Gothic *palace of the Major Council*. The earliest reference to this building is in a document from 1303. The palace was renewed and enlarged in 1487 as a Gothic and Renaissance building. As the front was designed by the local master Paskoje Miličević, it probably looked like the front of the Sponza Palace which was built by the same master. The front was decorated with valuable statues.

Many foreign and local masters worked on this important public palace. Radivoje Bogosalić and Leonard Petrović constructed the building, whereas Rade Ivanov and Marin Radetić decorated the interior. Direct connection with the Rector's Palace existed on the first floor level. Over the doorway is the inscription: OBLITI PRIVATORUM PUBLICA CURATE - Forget private business, care for public affairs. In the course of the 18th century the palace was also used as a public theatre. It was completely destroyed by fire in 1816, and the new town hall was built in the same place in 1882, in Neo-Gothic style. The new theatre was built within this complex, and the City coffee house was built in the 20th century.

The House of the Main Guard was built in the Gothic style close to the Palace of the Major Council. This building was of a very great importance for the safety of the city, as it was the residence of the admiral, supreme commander of the armed forces. The ground-floor of the building was reconstructed in early 18th century, and the monumental Baroque portal was built between 1706 and 1708. The author of the reconstruction was the Venetian architect Marino Gropelli, who had also designed the new Baroque church of St. Blasius.

Opening of
Dubrovnik Summer Festival,
the principal summer festival
in Croatia

The Little Onofrio fountain, 15th century

Bonino di Milano, Roland's column (15th century)

Close to the Guard-House is *the Little Onofrio's Fountain*. After the completion of the aqueduct, its builder Onofrio della Cava set two public fountains at the western and eastern ends of Placa. The Big Onofrio's Fountain, which is also a water reservoir, is at the western end close to the Pile Gate, while the Small fountain was placed at the eastern end to supply water to the market place which was in the Luža Square.

The Little Onofrio's Fountain was built in 1438, and is masterly combination of function and decoration. The sculptures were made by Pietro di Martino of Milan. In the Middle Ages water had a religious significance, so this Fountain was for the use of Christians only. Close by was another fountain for the use of the Jewish community of Dubrovnik - *Žudioska česma*. This one was later shifted to the Pile Gate.

In the middle of the Luža Square is a high and slender stone column with flag-staff, decorated with the figure of the *legendary medieval knight Roland*. The column was set up in 1418, and the flag of the free Republic with the image of its patron saint on white ground streamed from the column for four centuries. The column is Gothic in style and was carved by the sculptor Bonino of Milan with the help of local craftsmen. The figure of the proud knight is a fine example of monumental Gothic

66

sculpture. It is an interesting question how this knight, the symbol of north European cities, came to southern Adriatic. Although tradition has it that this knight defended Dubrovnik from the raids of the Saracen pirates, the explanation of the riddle is of political character. Dubrovnik was in 15th century protected by Sigismund, the King of Hungary, Croatia and Bohemia, later also the German Emperor. Sigismund was also Margrave of Brandenburg, a province where such columns were common. Thus Roland of Dubrovnik is symbol of loyalty to Sigismund, whose protection was crucial in the strife against Venice. Roland formerly looked east towards the Custom-Office, but it was often moved. In 1825 the column was blown down by a gale and was kept in a store for half a century. When the column was set up again, it was turned so that Roland faces north. It is of interest that the length of his forearm was taken for a measure - the ell of Dubrovnik, which is 51.1 cm.

The Bell Tower with clock was built in 1444 right in the axis of the Placa. It is 31 metres high and together with the Tower Minčeta and the Roland's Column is one of the symbols of the free city state. The bell tower was built by the local masters Grubačević, Utišenović and Radončić. Prior to the construction of this tower the city clock was on the Rector's Palace. The coloured brass face of the new clock with the hand showing the phases of the moon, and the two human figures which strike the bell announcing hours, were made by Luka, son of Admiral Miho Žugrović. A new plate with ciphers was made somewhat later by the painter Matko Junčić. The wooden figures were replaced by the famous horses, and in 1509 the noted bell-founder Ivan of Rab cast another bell with an epigraph by Ilija Lampridije Crijević. It was also hit by the earthquake, it lost its stability, it leaned and was in danger of falling. Therefore it was rebuilt in 1929 after the original drawings.

In the area between the Bell Tower and the Sponza Palace is *Luža*, the old bell-house. After a gunpowder explosion in the Rector's Palace the bells for

Luža, Bell Tower, House of the Main Guard

summoning the Major Council were moved from the Palace to Luža. The bells at Luža were also used as alarm bells to warn citizen in case of fire or other danger. Luža was built in 1463, and generally renewed in 1952. Beneath Luža is the inner city gate, built in the Gothic style, the Customs Gate, leading from Placa towards Ploče Gate or directly to the old port through the Fish Market Gate.

Following pages:
The square in front of Luža is
one of the most picturesque places.
From left: Sponza palace, Luža, Bell Tower,
House of the Main Guard, St. Blasius'

Close to Luža, on the left side of the square is the monumental Gothic-Renaissance *Sponza Palace*, one of the most beautiful in the city, which has preserved its original form. Its form suggests possible appearance of the majority of public and private palaces before the earthquake of 1667. Its name is derived from the word for the spot where rainwater was collected (*Spongia* - "alluvium"). In the time of the Republic this palace housed the custom office and bonded warehouse, hence it was often referred to as Divona (from *dogana* - "customs"). The palace also housed the mint, the bank, the treasury, and the armoury. The Sponza Palace was the seat of a number of state offices, important in the life of the Republic, which was based on commerce. This complex palace was designed by *protomagister* Paskoje Miličević. It is a large rectangular building with an inner courtyard. An open porch communicates with the square in front; another porch opens on the first floor towards the yard, and there is a shady porch on the first floor in front. The building is a mixture of Gothic and Renaissance styles, typical of all important palaces which were built on the east Adriatic coast at that time. The porch and the sculptural ornaments of the building were made after 1516 by the brothers Andrijić, masters from Korčula, and by other less known stone-cutters. A beautiful medal with Jesus' monogram and two angels was carved by the sculptor Beltrand Gallicus on the back wall. Individual custom bonded warehouses have names of saints inscribed in capital letters above their doors. The main inscription on the arch of the atrium from which a balance was suspended drew attention to the fact that the city measures were true: FALLERE NOSTRA VETANT; ET FALLI PONDERA: MEQUE PONDERO CVM MERCES: PONDERAT IPSE DEVS - Our weights do not permit cheating or being cheated. When I measure the commodities, the Lord measures with me. The Sponza palace was not damaged in the earthquake of 1667, and this fact probably saved the Republic. Affairs of state could continue notwithstanding heavy destruction. Members of the *Academia dei Concordi*, founded at the close of the 16th century by a group of poets, met in the large hall on the first floor. That was Dubrovnik's first institution of literary life.

Nowadays the Sponza Palace is the home of the most important cultural institution of Dubrovnik - *the Archive*. Previously, in the times of the Republic, the archives were kept in the Rector's Palace. Almost all documents that cover the period between the 12th century and the fall of the Republic are to be found there. More recent documents from the 19th and 20th centuries are also there. The wealth of records of all kinds make these archives one of the most important historical archives of the world. The archives contain 7000 volumes of manuscripts and about 100,000 of individual manuscripts. The earliest charter in the archives is from 1022. As early as 1278, the Republic introduced compulsory registration and filing of all public and private legal documents. The official languages of the documents were Latin and Italian, but many documents are in Croatian, also in Turkish, Spanish, Russian, New Greek and Arabic. Of especial value is the collection of statutory and law books, among them the Statutes of Dubrovnik of 1272. The records of the Chancellery and the Notaries of the Republic are all preserved, together with the copies all testaments, the protocols of all the three Councils of the Republic, official correspondence, records of voyages of all ships, cargo and passenger lists, and many other precious historical data from which the political, diplomatic and economic history of the Republic can be reconstructed, as well as a wealth of materials relating to the history of other countries and nations.

Right:
The Sponza Palace

Following page:
Interior court in Sponza palace

Close to the Town Hall (formerly the palace of the Major Council) is *the Rector's Palace*, an outstanding monument of secular architecture not only in Dubrovnik but on the whole Adriatic coast. This harmonious Gothic and Renaissance palace owes its present shape to many additions and reconstructions in its stormy history. From time to time it was destroyed or heavily damaged by fire, gunpowder explosions and earthquake. A defence building stood at the site of the present palace in early Middle Ages, and in the Statutes of 1272 it was referred to as *castrum*. In 1296 it was *castellum*. i.e. fortress. The term *palatium* - "palace" - occurs in the documents in 1349, and later the term *palazzo maggior*. As the documents sometimes specify its parts, it could be deduced that it was a building with corner towers, two wings and a high wall which enclosed the yard. The intent to embellish the building became manifest in the 15th century. This was certainly made easier because fires and gunpowder explosions had so seriously damaged the old building and its towers that it had to be

Semi-capital in relief from Rector's palace

Capitals from the front of Rector's palace

rebuilt practically from the foundations. After the fire of 1435 which gutted the building and its towers, the government decided to build a new, more beautiful palace. The job was entrusted to Onofrio della Cava of Naples, master builder who had previously built the aqueduct. The Rector's palace rose as a smart and harmonious two-story Gothic building, with a pillared porch between two side towers which are slightly higher. The column of the porch end in most beautiful capitals with figural representations. The sculptural ornaments of the palace, including the capitals, were made by master Pietro di Martino of Milan. Only a semi-capital with the figure of Aesculapius built into the southern angle of the porch, the capital with the scene of

Rector's palace,
15th century

Rector's palace, the bell

Bronze bust of
Dubrovnik's benefactor Miho Pracat,
in the atrium of the Rector's palace

the Judgement of Solomon (which is now in the City Museum), and four figural wall brackets in the front porch have survived to the present day. Although the arrangement of the figures was Gothic, they show evidence of early Renaissance spirit. A gunpowder explosion occurred in the armoury of the palace in 1463 and heavily damaged it. The renewal was entrusted the famous architect Michelozzo of Florence who was reconstructing the city walls at the time. It appears that his plans were too much in the style of the Renaissance for the tastes of the notoriously conservative Major Council because they rejected them on May 5, 1464. Michelozzo left Dubrovnik soon after, and the work was continued by other builders. The arches in the porch were reshaped according to the principles of the Renaissance with completely new Renaissance capitals. The modernisation of the sculptural decoration was probably the work of the Florentine master Salvi di Michele who directed the reconstruction from 1467 on. The main changes of Onofrio's building were made on the western and southern fronts where the former simple windows were replaced by large biforas, eight on the western front and three on the southern front. The biforas were carved by local masters Radivoj Bogosalić and Nikola Marković, while the relief ornaments on the portal were made by master Pavko Antojević Bogičević. New damage was caused by the earthquake of 1520. One of the masters who repaired it was Petar Andrijić of Korčula. The Palace suffered major damage in 1667. The southern front with biforas broke down, and this wing was rebuilt in the Baroque style. At the same time, a new Baroque flight of stairs was built in the atrium in place of the old one which was damaged, and a bell was set up on the first floor of the atrium. Its stand is decorated with rich rococo ornaments. It was connected to a clock mechanism below which struck the hours. On the ground-floor of the atrium, between two pillars in the eastern wing, the Senate had a monument erected in 1638 to Miho Pracat, a citizen of merit. He was a rich shipowner from Lopud who bequeathed his wealth to the Republic, and the only citizen (a commoner at that) whom the Republic had

Right: In front of Rector's palace

*Atrium of the
Rector's palace*

honoured with a monument in one thousand years of its existence. The bust was made by Pietro Giacometti of Recanati. The monument was damaged in the great earthquake, but it was repaired and returned to the same place in 1738. The eastern front, looking towards the harbour, underwent great changes after the earthquake. Originally representative in form, with a porch and a loggia, it was never restored to its previous shape. Owing to many misfortunes, the Rector's Palace became a unique building, harmoniously combining elements of Gothic, Renaissance and Baroque styles.

In addition to the Rector's Office and his private chambers, the reception and audience halls, the Palace was the seat of the Minor Council and of the state administration (the Secretary, the Notariate and the Cadastre), the armoury, the powder-magazine, the watch-house and the prison. The Rector, whose term of office was one month only, was not allowed to leave the Palace except on official business. He received the keys to the city gates every the evening during a ceremony for safe keeping. The ceremony was repeated every morning when he returned the keys. A row of stone benches are arranged along the western front wall under the porch. The Rector and the members of the Minor Council sat there on cushions, either to receive flag salute on St. Blasius day or to bid farewell to the ambassadors on their departure to distant countries. The Rector and his company used to watch carnival festivities from the same place too.

The Rector's Palace is the home to *the History Department of the Museum of Dubrovnik* today. The majority of the halls have style furniture so as to recreate the original atmosphere of these rooms. In addition to style furniture, here are numerous portraits and coats of arms of the noblemen, paintings of old masters, coins minted by the Republic, the original keys of the city gates, and a number of copies of important state documents.

Below: Rector's palace, Rector's office   *Right: The Cathedral*

Cathedral, St. John Nepomuk's altar (1758)

of Dubrovnik, proving as it does that Dubrovnik was an organized urban whole as early as the 7th century.

The Republic endeavoured to restore the ruined cathedral as soon as possible. An important role in these endeavours was played by Stjepan Gradić, one of the leading intellectuals of Dubrovnik, who was in Rome at the time employed as custodian and later rector of the Vatican library, but also in the role of unofficial ambassador of his native city of Dubrovnik to the Holy See. Gradić had many friends in Rome and he used his influence to find help for the rebuilding of his native city. His was the plan to renew the cathedral in the form of the Roman Baroque. With this in mind, he suggested that the Republic employ the famous Roman architect Andrea Buffalini of Urbino. Buffalini designed the new cathedral as a Roman Baroque church with three aisles and a cupola. The front of

Cathedral treasury, reliquary of the saint's head shaped like the crown of the Byzantine

The Cathedral of the Assumption of the Virgin was built in the 18th century after almost complete destruction in the earthquake of 1667 of the former 12th-14th century Romanesque cathedral. According to historical sources, the former cathedral was a magnificent basilica with a cupola, richly decorated with sculpture. According to tradition, part of the money to build the church was contributed as a votive gift by King Richard the Lion Heart having survived shipwreck near the island of Lokrum in 1192 on his return from the Third Crusade. During the restoration work in 1981, foundations of an earlier cathedral were discovered. Its architectural features suggest that it was built in the 7th century. This discovery gives a new dimension to the history

Cathedral, view towards the entrance

this church rises upon a flight of seven steps, and is articulated in a typical Baroque manner so as to emphasize the rich front and the concept of dynamic space with multiple contrasts of light. The protruding central part with the main portal is dominated by four high Corinthian columns. The upper half of the central part with a large Baroque window, shallow pillars and a strong triangular gable, rises above the attic. The left and right sides of the front have one floor only, articulated with pillars and deep niches with statues, and with a balustrade and statues of saints on top. The two smaller side entrances are considerably lower than the central one. The lateral walls of the church are articulated by small pillars and large semicircular Baroque windows. The aisles are separated from the nave by big columns. A slim Baroque cupola rises at the intersection of the nave and the transepts. The building of the church began in 1671 after Buffalini's plans. The first master builder was Paolo Andreotti of Genoa. He was followed by Pier Antonio Bazzi of Genoa, and friar Tommaso Napoli of Palermo. The new cathedral was finished in 1713 by the local architect Ilija Katičić. The cathedral has several fine late Baroque altars, such as the altar of St. Bernard built by Carlo degli Frangi, or the unique altar of St. John Nepomuk built of violet marble in northern Baroque style. This altar was a gift by the bishop of Sirmium Nikola Josip Gjivović from Pelješac, who was a counsel to the Austrian queen Maria Theresa. The treasury of Dubrovnik cathedral was one of the richest on the Adriatic coast, but it was badly damaged in the earthquake. The objects which could be saved from the ruins and the sites of the conflagration testify to the great art treasures that the churches possessed. Among the most precious objects in the treasury are the reliquaries of the head and the arm of the patron saint of Dubrovnik St. Blasius. The reliquary of his head, in the form of the.

*Cathedral
of the Assumption
of the Virgin, interior*

*Picturesque market
at Gundulić Square*

Byzantine imperial crown, is embellished with enamelled medals and precious stones. It is an outstanding example of goldsmith's work from 11th-12th century. The treasury has many reliquaries and church vessels from the 13th to the 18th century, some of them made by famous goldsmiths of Dubrovnik. An interesting detail testifies to the proverbial caution of the citizens. As treasury of the cathedral was also regarded as property of the Republic, access was possible only if three different keys were used simultaneously: one was kept by the archbishop, one by the cathedral rector, and one by the secretary of the Republic. The treasury also has a number of paintings of extraordinary value - from the Romanesque-Byzantine icon of the Virgin with Child from the 13th century to the paintings by Padovanini, Palma il Giovane, Savoldo, Parmigianino, P. Bordone and others. The big polyptych of the Assumption of the Virgin which adorns the sanctuary was made in Titian's workshop, possibly in part by Titian himself. This painting was moved to the cathedral from the church of St. Lazarus in Ploče, which was destroyed.

A detached polygonal *baptistery* building of red and white stone stood to the west of the cathedral, close to it, in the present Bunić square. The baptistery was built in 1326, and was the only part of the old cathedral complex to survive the earthquake. It was pulled down in 1830 by an arrogant Austrian military commander because it obstructed the view from the window of his residence.

A relatively spacious, picturesque square lies to the west of the cathedral - *Gundulićeva poljana*, surrounded with old stone houses. In the daytime it is a lively, coloured, rich market-place, and in the summer evenings it becomes an open-air stage for the summer festival. The square is dominated by the monument to Ivan Gundulić, the most famous poet of Dubrovnik, erected by the grateful citizens in 1892. The monument is the work of Ivan Rendić, one of the first modern Croatian sculptors. A full bronze figure of the great poet stands on a high pedestal; its four surfaces are decorated in relief

Above: Ivan Rendić, monument to Ivan Gundulić

Right: Baroque steps in front of the Jesuit church

with scenes from the epic poem "Osman", his most famous poem. The west side shows the old man Ljubdrag meditating upon Dubrovnik, from the eighth canto. The south side shows the priest Blaž blessing the Christian army, from the eleventh canto. The east side shows a scene from the ninth canto, in which Sunčanica, the principal woman character, is taken to the Sultan's harem, and the north side shows King Vladislav on horseback as victor over the Turks.

A monumental *Baroque flight of steps* leads from the south side of Gundulić square to Ruđer

Interior of the church of St. Ignatius (17th-18th century)

Bošković square and the *church of St. Ignatius* and the *Collegium Ragusinum*, the famous Jesuit school. This urban complex is considered by many as having greatest Baroque characteristics, not only in Dubrovnik but in whole Dalmatia. Dissatisfied with many Italian teachers who often came in conflict with the citizen of Dubrovnik, bishop Beccadelli asked in 1555 the newly founded Jesuit society to establish a college in the city. The idea was not put into effect immediately. It was not until 1647 that when the legacy of the Jesuit Marin Gundulić made it finally possible to start planning. The Jesuit rector Gianbattista Canali prepared plans in 1653 to regulate this old section of the city in order to built the Jesuit church and college. His plans included pulling down a whole complex of old houses. Some of the houses were bought off, but the earthquake of 1667 stopped all further work. It was continued only at the end of the century. The famous Jesuit architect and painter Ignazio Pozzo

was hired for the purpose. He started working on the church project in 1699 and finished it in 1703. The church of St. Ignatius was completed in 1725, and opened for worship in 1729. The articulation of its monumental Baroque front is reminiscent of the architectural concept which is also visible in the cathedral of Dubrovnik. The interior of the church shows similar features too. The sanctuary is decorated with illusionist Baroque frescoes by Gaetano Garcia, which display scenes of life of St. Ignatius, founder of the Jesuit society. The Jesuit College abuts at right angles against the front of the church. It was built according to the design by Ranjina and Canali and, with its neutral and severe lines, it only emphasizes the Baroque front of the church and the articulated broad flight of steps towards the city. The author of these extraordinary steps was the Roman architect Pietro Passalacqua. They were designed in 1738. Their architectural articulation and its effect it represents a far echo of the famous Roman steps leading from Piazza di Spagna towards the church Trinità dei Monti.

In the oldest part of Dubrovnik, the district called St. Mary which is to west of the Jesuit Church and College, is the *old grain store Rupe*.

Dubrovnik gave particular attention to reserves of grain - in case of siege or famine. Provisions of grain were as important as supplies of gunpowder. Therefore the city had several grain stores, Rupe ("pits") being the largest and the most interesting from the architectural point of view. This granary was built between 1542 and 1590. Fifteen deep, dry

Granary Rupe

cisterns with a capacity of 150 wagons of grain were bored in the living rock, and the two-floor building above was the horizontal storage area from where grain flowed into the cisterns through a system of openings in the floor and arches, or through channels in the wall.

Besides its intrinsic interest, the building is now used as *Ethnographic Museum*.

At right angles to Placa (Stradun) many small narrow streets run towards the north with numerous flight of steps ascending steeply to the northern section of the city walls. These picturesque little streets are cut by a long straight *Prijeko street*, which runs parallel to Placa. This part of the city has preserved its original picturesque outlook. Prijeko street links these urban surroundings - somewhat more humble, but equally attractive. This rather narrow but straight street is bounded in the west by the lateral wall of the Franciscan monastery and in the east the front of *the church of St. Nicholas*. This little church was built as early as the 11th century and is one of the oldest churches in Dubrovnik. This church of the seamen of Dubrovnik was reconstructed several times, and the present-day front is from the 16th century.

In the east part of the city, close to the walls is the large architectural complex of the *Dominican monastery*. This area is one of the most important architectural complexes of Dubrovnik and a major treasury of cultural and art heritage in Dubrovnik. The Dominicans established their monastery in Dubrovnik as early as 1225, but the building of the church and the monastery took much longer, so the church and the monastery building were completed in the 14th century. The place that the Dominicans chose for their monastery was strategically one of the most sensitive points in the defence of the city, so that as early as the 14th century the whole complex came was included within city walls, becoming their part. The church is one of the largest Gothic buildings on the east Adriatic coast. It is of simple architectural design: a hall

Dominican monastery, Lovro Dobričević, polyptych Baptism of Christ, 1448

with a pentagonal Gothic apse which is separated from the central area by three high openings with Gothic arches. The high outer walls of the church are bare of ornaments. The portal on the southern side has certain Romanesque elements, but in 1419 Bonino of Milan added to it a frame ending in a pointed Gothic arch. The interior is rich in stone church furniture, a pulpit, gravestones and Renaissance niches. The Monastery complex acquired its final shape in the 15th century, when the vestry, the chapter house and the cloister were added. The beautiful porches of the cloister were built between 1456 and 1483., They were built by the local builders: Utišenović, Grubačević, Radmanović and others from the designs of the Florentine architect Massa di Bartolomeo. The arches of the cloisters are closed by beautiful Gothic and Renaissance triforas. In the middle of the courtyard is a richly decorated cistern crown. The vestry was built in 1485 by the famous Dubrovnik architect Paskoje Miličević. The bell-tower was started by the architect Checo of Monopoli in the 16th century, but it was finished only in the 18th century. Although the complex of the Dominican Monastery has in some of its elements different style characteristics, from the Romanesque to the Baroque, it is a harmonious and logical architectural unit, but nevertheless predominantly Gothic and early Renaissance. A special treasure of this monastery is its library with over 220 incunables, numerous illuminated

*The cloister of the
Dominican monastery,
15th century*

Above: Dominican monastery, Nikola Božidarević, altar-piece Đorđić, The Virgin, detail, 16th century

Right: Ploče Gate

manuscripts, and a rich archive with precious manuscripts and documents. The art collection is very rich, and the best paintings of Dubrovnik school of the 15th - 16th centuries have a special place among them - works by Nikola Božidarević, Lovro Dobričević and Mihajlo Hamzić. Of foreign paintings, the painted crucifix by the noted Venetian painter Paolo Veneziano from the 14th century and the altarpiece of St. Magdalene, a work of Titian and his assistants from 1550 deserve especial attention.

Of the more recent Croatian painters, the altarpiece "Miracle of St. Dominic" by Vlaho Bukovac and paintings by Ivo Dulčić also deserve attention.

The eastern entrance to the city is protected by a complex of walls, towers and fortifications. As the detached fortress Revelin is also in front of the city walls, the eastern entrance consists of an outer and inner gate, *the Ploče Gate*. The inner gate is smaller, built in the Romanesque style; it is within the zone of the city walls and is protected by the high tower *Asimon* (Kula od Ploča), built in the 14th century. The outer gate near the south-eastern corner of the fortress Revelin and was built by Simeone della Cava in mid 15th century. This gate was widened in the 19th century. The stone bridge over the defence ditch was built in mid 15th century.

A large building which served as a *lazaretto* was situated in the region named Ploče close to the sea. Its purpose was to put in quarantine foreign sailors, travellers and merchants in order to prevent the spread of contagious disease and a possible epidemic. In the course of the 15th century large

Interior court and interior of the Art gallery

lazarettos were built in the region named Danče, to the west of the city, and in the 16th century such buildings were also provided on the island Lokrum. The Lazarettos at Ploče were built from late 16th to the 18th century. They were located at a suitable position along the former Trebinje road, where caravans from the Turkish hinterland came down. The building is composed of several parallel longitudinal rooms which one enters from the courtyard. Small watch-towers face the road. The Lazaretto building is very well preserved.

A stately stone palace in Frana Supila Way to the east of Ploče, built between the two world wars

inspired by the Renaissance and Gothic summer villas of the patricians, serves as the home of the *Gallery of Fine Arts*, one of the richest public collections of paintings on the Croatian coast. This gallery has many paintings from the 19th and 20th centuries, and particularly it exhibits paintings by the local painters - from Vlaho Bukovac to modern colourists. This Gallery arranges many exhibitions of national and international character, and is in this respect one of the most important national institutions of its kind in Croatia.

The *island of Lokrum*, covered with dense greenery, is situated near the shore to the east of the city. In

A motif from Lokrum

addition to a dense pine forest, Lokrum is rich in Mediterranean and sub-tropic vegetation, and because of extraordinary natural beauty it was declared a national park. In the south-eastern part of Lokrum, amidst dense vegetation, is an old *Benedictine monastery* from the 12th century, which was abolished by the French occupation during the reign of Napoleon. In 1859 the Archduke Maximilian of the House of Habsburg, the future Emperor of Mexico, converted the monastery into his summer residence, had it reconstructed in Neo-Gothic style, and added a high tower. After his death in Mexico the monastery changed many owners. Early in the 19th century the French had built *Fort Royal* on the highest peak of Lokrum, which now serves as a belvedere to many visitors.

Left: Palace of the Gallery of Fine Arts

The area to the west of the city walls is named *Pile*, after the western entrance to the city. The area right in front of the gate is *Brsalje*, today important crossroad and reception point for tourists. To the west of the fortress Lovrijenac is *Kolorina*, the oldest port in Dubrovnik. Close to Pile is *Gradac*, a large park which offers full view of the city and the open sea. Under the southern wall of Gradac, in the region named *Danče*, lazarettos were built in the 15th century to prevent the spread of plague and other epidemics. The rules of quarantine in Dubrovnik were very strict and the isolation of the sick was very long. Close to the lazarettos is the small *church of St. Mary* where some of the most beautiful paintings from the 15th and 16th century Dubrovnik school are kept - a polyptych by Lovro Dobričević and a triptych by Nikola Božidarević.

The deep and well protected *bay of Gruž* was formerly the site of the famous Dubrovnik shipyards, but in more recent times a new port was built there

mentioned villas, was built in the Renaissance style in 1578. These villas and others that the noblemen had built in Gruž, Lapad, Rijeka Dubrovačka, along the coast and on the islands of Koločep, Lopud and Šipan, their harmonious proportions, modesty, fine architectural details, gardens containing selected greenery, fruit trees and fish ponds - it all testifies to an exceptional culture of living in the times of the highest economic and political progress of the Republic.

The large, forested *Lapad peninsula* lies to the west of the historic centre of Dubrovnik is. Its highest peak is the hill Petka. Lapad is now a suburban area with accommodation

Left: Lovro Dobričević, St. Julian, detail of polyptych The Virgin with Child, church of St. Mary at Danče, 1465

Below: Church of St. Mary at Danče, Nikola Božidarević, triptych Virgin with saints, 1517

and an urban settlement developed close to it. *Gruž* was the suburban area where the patricians of Dubrovnik had their summer villas, many of them preserved to the present day. Three big villas are at the very end of the bay, which were built in the 16th century. The first one is the summer residence of Palatin Gundulić, built in 1527 in the Renaissance style with a chapel, a separate pavilion, gardens and a fish pond. Close to it Junije Bunić built his villa in 1550. The front of his residence with Gothic windows is one of the latest examples of conservative Gothic style in the region of Dubrovnik. The third, owned by Martin Bunić, and situated between the two above-

Petar Sorkočević's villa at Lapad

for tourists, hotels and other tourist services. In the past Lapad was the region of numerous Renaissance summer villas, of which certainly the most famous was the *mansion belonging to Petar Sorkočević*, situated at the very beginning of the peninsula, opposite Gruž.

It is situated at the foot of a wooded hill near the sea shore. It was built in the decades between 1520 and 1580 in a mixture of Gothic and Renaissance styles. It has Renaissance characteristics on the ground-floor, but the monoforas and the trifora on the first floor are Gothic. The first floor opens to a large terrace under which is a water cistern. The residence is surrounded by a high wall. The garden with lush vegetation has two parts on different levels and a large fish pond. The villa has a small protected garden with a chapel. *The Institute of Historical Science of the Croatian Academy of Science and Arts* is housed nowadays this villa.

The well-known *church of St. Michael* and *the old cemetery of the nobility* is located in Lapad. *The Church of the Virgin of Grace* is a votive church and it owns a rich and interesting collection of paintings of old sailing ships.

Following pages:

Lapad, Petar Sorkočević's villa
(first half of 16th century)

Sunset at Stradun

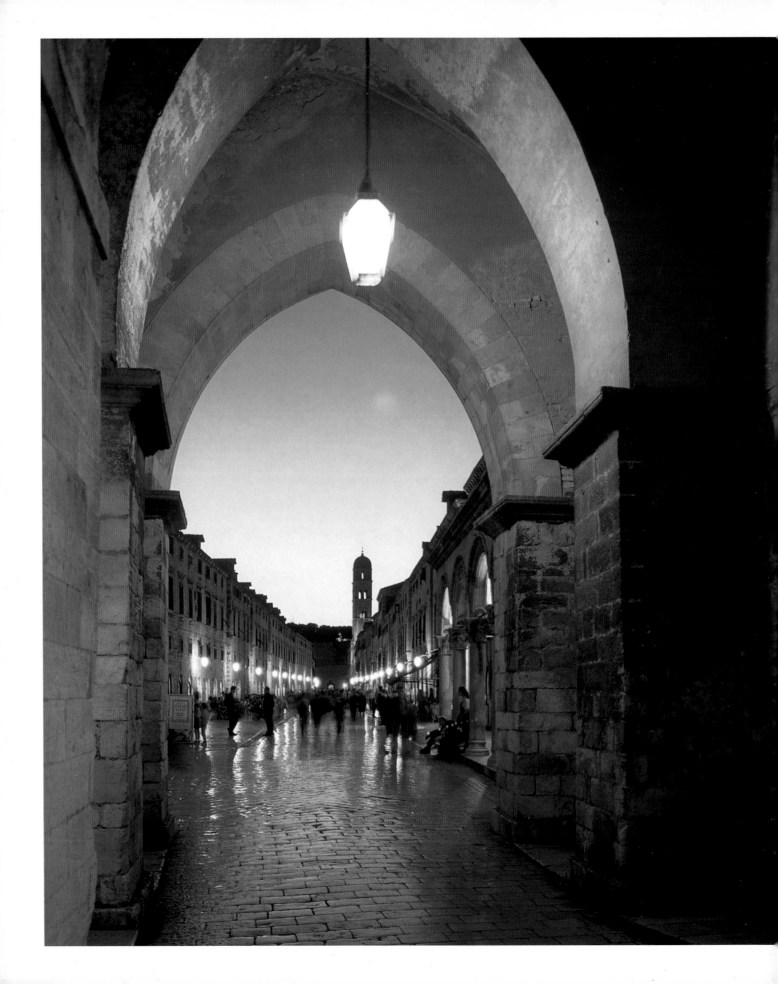